QUEEN WARRIOR

Crown Bound

KAREN GILLIAM

Scripture quotations taken from the Amplified® Bible (AMPC),

Copyright © 1954, 1958, 1962, 1964, 1965, 1987 by The Lockman Foundation

Used by permission. www.lockman.org

Heart Journal Image by PIRO4D from Pixabay

ISBN 978-1-950861-68-2
PRINTED IN THE UNITED STATES OF AMERICA

Cover Photo and About the Author Photo By Kate Singh

Disclaimer: This book contains content of a sensitive nature. There is shared information regarding cancer diagnosis and the transition of a spouse, which may be difficult to read. The author seeks to be transparent about the accounts of this journey in order to help others.

His Glory Creations Publishing, LLC
Wendell, North Carolina

DEDICATION

I dedicate this book to my husband, Brian Davis Gilliam, whom I shared this life with for 46 years. I didn't lose you because in the spirit realm I will see you again. Rest well in Paradise! I love you!

ACKNOWLEDGEMENTS

I would like to acknowledge God, who is the center of my life. You perfect everything that concerns me.

I also acknowledge my children, Shawn, Kevin and Brianna. Your lives are a reflection of your dad and I. I love you all and thank you for my "sugars!" We are #gilliamstrong

Thank you, Pastor Dan Thomas and Lady Shasa, for your spiritual guidance and prayers.

Thank you to all the prayer warriors who interceded for Brian and I.

Thanks to Coach Denise Walker of Armor of Hope for your coaching and my first writing experience.

Thank you also to Felicia Lucas and His Glory Creations Publishing Company for your professionalism and guidance.

Thank you LaLonnie Bell, my dear friend, for seeing me as a "Queen Warrior" and not a widow.

Table Of Contents

Introduction

D o you remember your wedding vows? The part about taking a husband/wife to have and to hold from this day forward, for better or worse, richer or poorer, in "sickness and in health," to love and cherish until we are parted by death. No one prepares us for what to do as a caregiver for your spouse when they become ill or is diagnosed with a terminal illness. At that moment, we've said the words, but what does it mean when faced with the task? Unless you have been trained in a medical profession, you sort of wing it.

I vowed 43 years ago to take care of my husband in "sickness and in health," but I never knew what that would mean until the fall of 2020. What I didn't know, I quickly learned. He needed me in so many ways. As he took this journey, so did I.

Not only did I not know how to care for him on this journey, I also had to learn about taking care of his final wishes, his business affairs, and passing along his legacy. I was in a new season of my life. After 43 years of marriage, I was now on my own.

In this book, I will carry you on our journey. I will share how God orchestrated every aspect of it. This transparency will unveil what to do, how to do it, and reflection questions to get you thinking about your own journey.

It will show you how God is always with you. He won't leave or forsake you. I wrote this book to help as many women as possible. I want women to be able to navigate through the circumstances by knowing what to expect. I do not want them to feel abandoned and uncertain, nor be classified as a widow. It is my desire that no one succumbs to the perception of a "widow." Widows are seen as distraught, lonely, depressed, and weak. To sum it up, they are viewed as an emotional wreck.

As a believer, I had the emotions, but the emotions didn't have me. I trusted God and knew I had a purpose to share with others on how to go on. A friend of mine saw me not as a widow but as a "Queen Warrior." The definition is a female ruler of an independent state. This power is inherited at birth. When we become born again and receive Christ, we inherit the kingdom of God as heiresses (Romans 8:17-18 and John 1:12-13, Amplified). A queen knows how to maneuver her way (read the Book of Esther). Queens do not conform to this world. She is and can do all things through Christ from which comes her help.

A warrior takes a stand, willing to work hard to get what we want, defend ourselves, and others when we need to do so. A warrior values strength. Our strength then allows us to stand in defense for others who may not be able to. She knows her value and will not give up, give in, or quit.

My heartbeat has gone on, but my heart is still beating, which means God has a purpose for me. Come take the journey with me. You are a Queen Warrior. God gave you an inherent gift that is only found in your strength. Proverbs 31:25, Amplified, "She is clothed with strength and dignity, and she laughs without fear of the future."

QUEEN = Dignity
WARRIOR = Strength

CHAPTER ONE

My Journey – The Beginning (The Big Transition)

My husband and I took our vows over 43 years ago. We were a military family traveling with our three children across the country and abroad. When Brian retired, we decided to move back to the East Coast where we both grew up. We lived in our home state of Virginia for a while. Then, after I accepted a position in North Carolina, we moved to Raleigh. After twelve and a half years in North Carolina, the start of our journey transitioned us from Raleigh to Vancouver, Washington. We had our three children who had families of their own. Those who know me best know that I refer to our eleven grandchildren as "grandsugars." Do you know why? It is because they are "sweet" as can be!

The decision to transition did not come easy, and I'll give you one guess who was holding out. We traveled to the Pacific Northwest at least once or twice a year. Each time, returning to North Carolina was harder on me than Brian. The "sugars" were growing up. I wanted to be a part of their lives. God knew the desires of my heart, and I knew my prayers were heard. I had to learn that God's timing was always best.

We built our home from the ground up and had lived there since 2012. We were empty nesters but enjoyed our lives with each other and our dog, Gigi. Our children and their families lived in Washington state where they pretty much grew up when Brian was stationed in Portland, Oregon. Brian and I had several conversations about moving back to Washington, but he would always give me "reasons" why it wasn't the best decision. He would say the cost of living was too high in Washington. How can you put a dollar value on being with family especially your children and grands?

Time moved on after each conversation, but my prayers were always to move back. We even drove cross country, the summer of 2020, for one of our grandkids' high school graduation celebrations. We were cautious because of the Covid pandemic but made the trip smoothly. One Sunday evening in September of 2020, Brian was sitting out on the porch with Gigi while I was preparing dinner. He called me to come there and surprised me with an idea to sell the house and move back to Vancouver, Washington. I remember saying to him, "Don't play with me!" He asked me to research about selling the home and look into moving expenses. I was elated and thanked God because I knew He put the idea into Brian's head. It was an answer to prayer, but there was a purpose behind the transition.

There was lots to do for this transition, and it was our goal to move back to Washington before Thanksgiving because the weather would change and make traveling across the country challenging. Every aspect of this transition was orchestrated by God. God prepared me for it as I attended a daily morning prayer group on Facebook, and my faith grew deeper for what was coming. My pastor gave me a word from the Lord that this would be the greatest transition of our lives.

As you might imagine, I went to work on selling our home and getting information about the cost of the move. God stepped in again with the choice of realtors to handle the sale. I was looking to have a friend sell our home, but the agency wanted us to do some prep work we felt would take too much time. We were on a time schedule and needed to sell quickly. We were in a seller's market, and properties were selling fast, but the window of opportunity according to the realtor was closing because of the holidays approaching. The decision was made for the selling price of our home and preparation was in motion. Before we knew it, the house sold in a matter of days. It was a cash offer above the asking price. We now had to make arrangements for our household to be packed and shipped to Vancouver. Brian and I were grateful.

Everything seemed to be going as scheduled. We had to stay in a hotel after the household was packed and shipped. We thought it would be just for a few days. Once closing took place, we would be leaving for the Pacific Northwest. Neither of us saw the next chapter of this journey unfolding. We were faced with challenges that caught us by surprise, but God knew the plan.

REFLECTIONS

What are or have you faced during a major transition?

_____

_____

_____

_____

_____

_____

_____

What emotions or feelings did you experience?

_____

_____

_____

_____

_____

_____

_____

What was the turning point when you knew God was with you during the transition?

_____

_____

_____

_____

_____

_____

_____

CHAPTER TWO

My Journey – The Beginning (The Diagnosis)

Every marriage faces challenges. Brian and I had our share during our 43 years. My thoughts at first about our "greatest transition of our lives" were that it would be smooth or at least minimal challenging. I had thoughts God would take care of everything, and we would enjoy the journey.

The one challenge we faced that caught us by surprise was after our annual flu shots. Brian found a lump under his arm and was experiencing pain. Brian was hardly ever sick. He had headaches, colds, and one knee surgery. He was in very good health as he aged. He never liked being "health conscious" because he loved his desserts. He said, "All the milk I drink, I'm healthy." He always had milk with his desserts. When he was younger, he would drink milk after playing basketball. Who does that?

I took Brian to urgent care to be seen about the lump. It was recommended that he have a mammogram. All the tests in the initial diagnosis showed it was an infection. Medication was prescribed and the lump gradually disappeared.

The next two weeks brought additional challenges with the closing of our home. There was poor communication between our mortgage company, our attorney, and the court system in receiving the permission to sell. This was due to us filing for a chapter thirteen bankruptcy, which held up the sale's process. Our realtor was concerned that the cash offer buyer would back out of the purchase. I was relentless with all involved to resolve the issue. God gave me such boldness to effectively communicate and not settle for what they would tell me. I spoke declarations of faith that we would have favor with all parties involved. I was careful not to forget that Brian and his health were always my top priority.

By this time, we were still living in a hotel and the time for us to leave for Washington was getting closer. Brian started to have abdominal pains, and it was at times very excruciating. One morning, in the wee hours, I had to take Brian to the emergency room at one of our local hospitals. It was difficult to see him in so much pain and not be able to help him. My help was to pray while in the waiting room. Due to the COVID restrictions, I couldn't go back with him initially. A nurse came for me when he was in a room. He was given pain meds while waiting for the test results.

The doctor entered the room to give us the results. Brian was in less pain than when we arrived. No medication could take away the pain of what the doctor shared with us. Her bedside manner was nonchalant as she spoke these words, "I'm sorry I have to tell you this, but you have cancer." I immediately looked at Brian who was in disbelief. When the doctor left the room to make arrangements with an oncologist, I focused on him. He broke down in tears and said, "I guess it's my turn." I knew what he meant because his father had died of cancer the same year we were married. I immediately responded, "Whose report are we going to believe?" We believe the report of the Lord. By Jesus' stripes we are healed. We won't believe this bad report."

The human side of me wanted to cry, and I did for a moment. I cried when he cried, but God's strength in me consoled him and spoke words of faith and not doubt or fear. When I would speak words of belief, he would sometimes repeat after me.

Time was of the essence. Questions flooded both of our minds of how everything would work out. I encouraged Brian to focus on his health and getting stronger, and I would focus on him as a priority. Then, there was the matter concerning our house sale and moving. Brian was convinced he could have done things differently to avoid his diagnosis.

The day I shared the diagnosis with our children and other family members is somewhat of a blur. I couldn't share the news in person because they were all in other states. My daughter said I sent a text message in our family chat. She recalls the date and what she was doing at the time. I know I kept the positivity and had them thinking good thoughts about the situation. We created the hashtag, #gilliamstrong, to remind us that we are strong. We stood together as a family, and Brian had the love and support of each of us to see him through this ordeal.

I was grateful for the immediate appointments with the oncologist and the plan of treatment she felt was best. Brian was diagnosed with Hodgkin's lymphoma, a type of blood cancer. We were not going to be able to leave at our anticipated time for Washington because Brian had to have at least 6 treatments and be stable before she could approve a cross country move. This was pushing our departure back until January of 2021. We continued to live in the hotel. Brian's first chemotherapy treatment was the week of Thanksgiving. My visits were either limited or not allowed due to Covid. We would FaceTime or talk on the phone just to stay in touch.

The holidays were not the same as in previous years. Thanksgiving dinner was after my visit with Brian. I picked up a Thanksgiving meal from Cracker Barrel and headed back to the hotel. Christmas was quiet as well. Brian and I celebrated at the hotel. I got a decorated mini tree and stockings for our room. He rested for his next treatment which meant we would not be together for New Year's Eve. Each time Brian went to be admitted to the hospital, he was given a Covid test. This time the test was positive, but he had no symptoms. Therefore, he was admitted to the Covid floor for his chemotherapy treatments. He said it was lonely on that floor since no visitors were allowed up. My heart ached for him being there, especially during the holiday.

I started to feel like I had the flu. I ran a temperature and my body ached. I had no sense of taste or smell. Everything I ate tasted horrible. I was extremely tired and spent New Year's Eve on Zoom with my family across the country for a celebration of the new year. Both of my Covid tests came back negative, but the doctor told me I had the symptoms. Regardless of the tests results, I needed to quarantine. The new year of 2021 was not looking too great. I still relied on my faith and trusted God. Sometimes you must look passed what you see with your natural eyes and focus on the promise God gave you. I believed and trusted God that what He promised Brian and I would manifest.

This battle Brian was fighting, I was fighting too. I held on to God's Word more and more. My children, family members and close friends were my rocks here on earth. I found myself comforted by God's Word and my strength growing for what was ahead. "The Lord will accomplish that which concerns me" (Psalms 138:8, Amplified), was a scripture I repeated constantly. My vow to take care of Brian in sickness and in health. Just as God promises, I also promised. It was my solemn promise and personal commitment to be his caregiver.

REFLECTIONS

What were your initial feelings/emotions when you received the news of the diagnosis?

_____

_____

_____

What thoughts went through your mind as things developed?

_____

_____

_____

Who did you talk to for comfort? Did your spiritual relationship bring you comfort?

_____

_____

_____

CHAPTER THREE

My Journey – The Caregiver

The role of a caregiver was new to me. I appreciated my sister-in-loves for their advice and encouragement. Brian's sister, Gail, was a medical assistant for over 30 plus years and my brother's wife, Lisa a caregiver for several family members during terminal illnesses and injuries. I admired both of them for their dedication to caring for others. I was about to embark on a new season of my life as Brian's caregiver and at times wondered if I could.

The reason I say that is because I struggled with caring for our children when they were sick with childhood illnesses. They knew to call Brian when their tummies would hurt and when they would vomit. I didn't like to visit people in hospitals, especially the emergency room because I never knew what I might see. I had unsettling feelings about blood and bodily functions. In my early years as a preteen, I witnessed family members who had terminal diseases, which left indelible impressions on me.

Even with the advice from my sister-in-loves, it wasn't until I was in the role of a caregiver that I developed knowledge and skills that made Brian's days better. Brian had good and bad days. Chemotherapy can take its toll on a person. He had days when he was irritable and stubborn. There were great days when he was laughing and telling stories I had heard several times in our years together, but I enjoyed them. The oral and chemotherapy medications made him tired. He slept a lot and even apologized when he couldn't stay awake. I reassured him I would be right there when he woke up.

The hospital and doctor's staff were excellent in their care with Brian. He was known for his humor. He loved telling them jokes and always tried to get what he wanted for his meals. I communicated with the staff to ensure that when he was home, which was the hotel, I could care for him properly. I asked questions about his diet and exercise. Now, as you can imagine, he would do better for them than with me. I also did a lot of reading and research on medications and treatments so I could be an advocate for him.

I maintained a positive and grateful attitude. When anyone would ask how I was doing, I responded, "I'm great and grateful!" I always communicated with Brian about maintaining a positive mental attitude to help with his healing. We prayed and read scriptures together. At the hospital and hotel, I played healing music with scripture readings.

When I wasn't his caregiver or advocate, I was in my other roles. We were still in negotiations for the sale of the house. The mortgage company started playing games to stall the sale. I became relentless in taking care of business to ensure when the time came, we would be ready to move to Washington. I developed boldness as a prayer warrior, interceding for Brian's healing. I learned to be "thick-skinned" when I needed to be, especially when Brian would lash out at me. I couldn't take things personally because I knew it wasn't the person I loved.

Now, about the sale of our home. I saw the hand of God move and grant us favor. On a day when Brian was very weak and had to be hospitalized, the buyer's attorney contacted me that the mortgage company would not cooperate in providing the documents needed for closing. I assured the attorney I would speak with them after Brian was settled. They were ready to close, and everything had been done except the payoff from the mortgage company. Once Brian was admitted and care was being administered for him, I went to call the mortgage company. The person I spoke with said it would take seven days before they could release the mortgage payoff. I immediately explained what he was saying was unacceptable. I asked to speak to a supervisor. Because he was working from home, he did not have immediate access. I told him I would call back every hour until I spoke to someone in authority.

Finally, I spoke with a supervisor. I kept myself calm but poured out my heart to him about what was going on. He quoted policies and procedures. I knew I needed to get back to Brian, and I told the supervisor I expected him to look for a loophole in the company's policies and procedures. I believed we could get this resolved. When you think about it, why would they stall on getting paid? I hung up and prayed before returning to Brian's room. I put it in God's hands. I returned to Brian's side and the doctor said that he was dehydrated and was going to stay over so they could administer fluids. Brian was not happy about having to stay but reassured him that it was for the best, and he would feel much better once he received the fluids.

At 4:30 p.m. that day I received a text from the buyer's attorney to call her. I told Brian I had to go call the attorney. I had updated him and asked him not to worry about what was going on. When I spoke to the attorney, she said they had received the payoff document they needed to close. She was sending the documents electronically for me and Brian's signature. The filing of the closing with the court would be that day by 5:00 pm. I was relieved and immediately signed and returned the documents. The filing with the court happened at 4:50 pm that day! Yes, God showed up and worked out the details while I prioritized to be with Brian. Our realtor was surprised, but he was a believer and realized God stepped in for us. I will never forget when I told Brian the good news that the sale was done. He shouted, "Hallelujah!" He also would say, "Unbelievable!" over and over, which was referencing everything up to this point of the journey.

Yes, it was unbelievable but not impossible. Some people might look at our journey and think it was impossible. It was unbelievable to go from having a cash offer for the house a few short days after being on the market. It was unbelievable we found favor with the court and mortgage company, unbelievable we lived in our house with bare essentials and a hotel for almost 3 months, unbelievable we both experienced Covid, and unbelievable Brian was diagnosed with cancer and yet the "unbelievable" made us more of believers in God and the power of our faith. There is nothing impossible for God.

It was because of my prayer times, journaling, scripture reading, and singing praises to God that I grew stronger in Him. Yes, I cried. At times, I was on my face before God. There was even a time when I questioned God. I asked, "Why?" The word I received was in Deuteronomy 11:22, Amplified. He said, I was to be careful to keep this commandment, which He was commanding me to do. I was to love the Lord my God, walk by living each and every day in His ways, and hold tightly to Him. The days following I didn't question, and I did not get mad with God. I'm not perfect, but I'm perfectly made in the image of God.

I would often reflect on the days of this journey. When Brian would question what he could have done differently to have avoid his diagnosis, I would question what I could have done differently in what I did in caring for him. I showed up every day for him. I made it my mission that he was receiving the best care, and I kept trusting God. So, I wouldn't have done anything differently. In the days ahead, I became Brian's voice, speaking on his behalf as I know he would.

REFLECTIONS

How would you say you were prepared to be your spouse's caregiver?

_____

_____

_____

What action steps did you take to be the best you could as a caregiver?

_____

_____

_____

If you had to do it over again, what would you do differently?

_____

_____

_____

CHAPTER FOUR

My Journey – Advocate (Becoming His Voice)

S tepping into the role of an advocate for Brian was a major shift in our relationship. Brian was a person who was driven by results. He was strong-willed in his personality. As a career military person, he was very disciplined in getting things done. He was a person who liked order. He would say, "If you take something from somewhere, be sure you put it back in the same place a person had it." I had to grow into his way of being because I was more of a spontaneous, accepting, and carefree person. They say opposites attract and I believe that was the case with us. In relationships, we tend to be attracted to characteristics we do not have personally in our mate. We complimented each other. I helped him be a more gentle person, and he taught me how to be more confident and independent.

Now, I was able to be confident and independent as his advocate. As his health deteriorated, Brian relied on me quite a bit. He wanted me to be with him as early as I could and stay as long as I could. No matter when I got there or when I left, he would be sad when I wasn't around.

During times of his physical or mental weaknesses, I had to step up and make sure he was being properly cared for. There were moments he was incoherent. His short term and sometimes long-term memory loss made him vulnerable. I made sure to communicate with the staff and asked to make sure I was included in the decisions about Brian's care.

I would spend time at home or in his room looking up research on his illness. Whenever medication was given, I researched the medication and asked questions about findings of side effects. I wasn't trying to undermine the knowledge or credibility of the medical staff. I was "being Brian" who would ask questions until he felt good about the situation. Even after that, he would ask me what I thought. On one occasion, he was asked about considering a clinical trial. He said he didn't want to be an experiment and refused. I did talk with the doctor about this trial, and she said it was an option, but there was no guarantee it would be effective. She felt confident the original plan of treatment was best.

My role of an advocate was more after our transition to Washington. Once we were here, Brian spent more time in hospitals than in North Carolina. When he was hospitalized the last time before he passed, I was more visible with the medical staff because the Covid restrictions were not as strict. There were still only two visitors who could be assigned to him and that was me and our daughter. I worked closely with a case worker assigned to Brian about his treatment in the hospital and his proposed home care. Even though Brian had an excellent medical staff, I took care of him as he needed. The staff had several patients to attend to, and I only had him. I surprised myself when I learned from observation how to care for him, but I was also able to help strengthen his memory by playing games to help exercise his brain.

I believe the lesson I learned from being Brian's advocate and caregiver is to be and do what's best for the person you love. It is this time that you put yourself aside and fulfill the vow you took when you married. All depends on their state of health as to how much of an advocate you will be.

One night, my phone rang. It was Brian calling to let me know the power had gone out at the hospital. He was concerned that no one could help him because there was no power in the hospital. I reassured him I would find out what was going on. He said that there were no lights in the hallway, and everything was pitch black. I asked him could I call him back after I investigated what was going on. He reluctantly agreed, but I could tell he didn't want me to hang up. He didn't want to be alone in the dark. I told him to look at the clock on his phone, and he could expect me to call him back within 15 minutes. He said okay, and I immediately called the hospital. The switchboard operator listened attentively as I explain what happened when Brian called me. She told me the power was not out. If it were to ever go out, they have backup generators.

She then connected me to the nurses' station on Brian's floor, and I explained to the nurse what Brian had told me. She assured me she would go and see what was going on, and she would call me back. As a matter of fact, she would call me from his room. Minutes later she called me from his room and said the television was off, and one of the other nurses must have turned off his lights because he was asleep. He continued to tell her there was a power outage and she kept reassuring him that they had power. After all that, the only thing he said to me was that I didn't call back in fifteen minutes. So, you see, no one knows what you will face as a caregiver. Just as Brian relied on me with the smallest detail, it wasn't small to him. You must be available to face anything.

It is a physically and mentally draining task to be a caregiver. There were nights I would come home exhausted, but I was up to do what I needed to the very next day. I would pray daily for physical and mental strength. I also prayed for the medical staffs who cared for Brian. I didn't hesitate to compliment them and thank them for what they were doing for him. If on occasion when Brian was being stubborn, I would talk to them outside his room to reassure them not to take it personally. They are trained for that, but they are still human.

During my journey I kept a journal. I tried to write something in it daily, but sometimes I failed to. I will share some of those entries with you in the last section of the book. Keeping a journal helped me to reflect on the day, keep an attitude of gratitude, and strengthen my memory. It was also one of the reasons I decided to write this book. As I read back through the days I wrote in my journal, I knew it was important to share my journey with others, especially women who may experience the same journey. I thank God for sustaining me through this journey. I could see His hand sustaining me one day at a time.

REFLECTIONS

How do you find yourself being the voice of your loved one?

_____

_____

_____

_____

_____

_____

_____

What are you doing to keep yourself strong?

_____

_____

_____

_____

_____

_____

_____

Share what happened in your situation where you had to be the "voice."

_____

_____

_____

_____

_____

_____

_____

CHAPTER FIVE

My Journey – Taking One Day at a Time

The day came when we could take the trip cross country to Vancouver, Washington. Brian and I were excited he had stabilized to be able to travel. He was given instructions on how to weather the trip, and he was already scheduled to resume his final treatments in Seattle the second week of February. We picked up our son, Kevin, at the airport the day before we were to leave. Kevin offered to come and help with the drive since Brian was limited in driving.

The next morning, we ventured out on our cross-country trip. We quickly realized each of us had our own best time to drive. Kevin liked the mornings, Brian took the afternoons, and I finished the day in the evenings. We averaged ten to twelve hours a day, but remember we had to do the southern route because we left in January, and the weather would have been very challenging going through the central part of the country, through the mountains the Dakotas, Idaho, and Oregon. We arrived the first week in February to start a new chapter in Vancouver, WA.

We were elated to be with our family. I truly believe being around those we loved helped Brian with his recovery. He had three more chemotherapy treatments in Seattle, and we were back to being apart when he had to stay for four days at a time because of Covid and hospital visitation restrictions. The drive was almost three hours one way. As soon as I would leave Brian, I looked forward to coming up and staying overnight in Seattle because he had a shot treatment the next day in the hospital. The last chemotherapy session was the weekend of Easter. We were both excited for him to "ring the bell," which symbolized that he was done with chemotherapy treatments. I videotaped this milestone in his journey and sent it out to everyone in the family and on social media. We both cried, and Brian continued saying, "Unbelievable!"

Up to this point, we were staying with our daughter, son-in-love and their family. Now was the time to find our home and let Brian enjoy his recovery. I had been searching for homes all along and realized Brian no longer could climb stairs. We were accustomed to having a two-story home but changed so Brian wouldn't have to worry about stairs. We were happy when we came across a home we both loved. The best part was the landlord knew Kevin from playing basketball with him. We immediately contacted him to let him know we wanted the house. He called while we were watching the Super Bowl to ask if we were still interested in his house. It was ours!

Preparations for the move-in came. Our family helped, and we felt so at home and grateful for Brian's recovery. Remember, I said Brian was a storyteller. He had a story for everything. While unpacking and arranging furniture in our new home, he shared so many stories. I loved how the grandkids and even our kids were mesmerized. Our kids had heard some of these stories many times before, but this was a special time of bonding and celebrating Brian's recovery.

We enjoyed being back together! We took "one day at a time," showing gratitude to God for the steps we had taken. God sustained us through the known and unknown. I remained grounded in His Word and found peace in my prayer and meditation times. Relying on God prevented me from going through burnout, both physically and mentally. I trusted Him so much. In my prayer time in the mornings, we sang a song about this day is the best day of my life. I spoke that every day, and I encouraged Brian to say daily, "Today and everyday I'm getting better and better!"

Brian had an opportunity to enjoy our home for about a month. After moving in, he had two sessions in Seattle. We weren't sure why his knees were weakening, and eventually he had to walk with a cane or walker. We knew the doctors said recovery was going to take time. In the natural, it seemed as though Brian was getting weaker. I still relied on my faith and trusting God.

I remember Mother's Day. That year was the first time I had been with the kids and grands in a long time on that holiday. Our daughter and son-in-love hosted the Mother's Day celebration at their home. Everyone was there, and I felt special. We did a zoom meeting with my siblings, had some great food, and special presentations were given by our kids and grands. Our daughter went first, presenting a framed picture of her with our sons. Each of them wrote special words to me. Our granddaughter presented me with a beautiful collage of all the "sugars." Each one of them came and hugged me. The tears were flowing all the more because I loved that we were all together.

Brian was getting tired, so we came home. He wanted to rest in bed, and I was in the front room watching television. I can't remember how long before I heard the most terrifying scream from Brian, and I immediately ran to the room to find Brian convulsing. He was having a seizure, and I called 911. He was taken to the hospital, not knowing much about where he was. It was as if his memory had been erased.

The doctors ran a CAT scan and other tests. The neurologist on duty in the emergency room told me it looked as if the lymphoma had traveled to his brain and was very aggressive. My first thoughts were, "How is that possible, after receiving a clean bill of health Easter weekend? Did the lymphoma hide out and decide to attack his brain?" Once again, I didn't want to believe the report they were sharing with me. Brian was transferred to a hospital in Oregon where he was seen by a specialist.

A few weeks after his admission to the hospital, the specialist wanted to prepare me for the worst and suggested I prepare the family. I insisted they maintain treatment, and I was not going to prepare my family. That day, our grandson was having his 18th birthday, and it was senior night at his high school. After getting the news, I didn't know how I was going to keep this from showing on my face. Brian was resting well when I left. As I walked to meet our family, I prayed and ask God to give me strength because that night was special to our grandson. Before leaving Brian's room, I set his Ipad to play healing scriptures and music. He slept most of the time, but it was important I did that for him.

The grace of God was with me that night. I was able to walk onto the court and hug our grandson along with his parents and other grandparents. God and I pulled it off and no one were the wiser. When I got home late that night, all kinds of thoughts ran through my mind. Was I prepared to live without Brian? Did he have everything for me after he passed? I wasn't doubting God, but when the doctor said he only gave him a week, at the latest, I was believing for a miracle. What if my idea of a miracle and God's are different? I thought.

The week turned into almost seven weeks before Brian passed away. The doctor was surprised but I wasn't. Our daughter and I were the only visitors he could have, so for Father's Day, we made it the best. Our daughter came in the morning, and I stayed home to prepare one of his favorite dinners. The nurses were impressed at how we celebrated Brian being a great dad and pappy. There were balloons, cards, special treats, and dinner could be smelled throughout the seventh floor. I even had to give my recipe for cornbread to a couple of the nurses. He was able to FaceTime with our sons and grands.

Before I went home, he wanted to record special messages for two of our grandsons who had big games coming up. I shared those recordings with them, and they both have them saved on their phones. I believe on a few occasions they play the recording for inspiration. One day at a time were the best days we had with Brian!

REFLECTIONS

What are you doing or have done to keep hope alive for your loved one?

_____

_____

_____

_____

_____

_____

_____

What does "one day at a time" mean to you?

_____

_____

_____

_____

_____

_____

_____

What did you do when you felt your faith wavering?

_____

_____

_____

_____

_____

_____

CHAPTER SIX

My Journey – The Final Transition (How I Let Go)

As I think back on this journey, I always believed Brian would be healed on this side of heaven and come back home. He had been in the hospital a month. I was by his side every day. Brian had already overcome what the doctor told me about preparing the family. The doctor was surprised but was glad to see Brian better.

It was a day before my birthday, and he asked me what I wanted. Without hesitation, I told him, "Having you come home would be the best birthday present ever." Plans were being made to bring Brian home the following week. I was working with the case worker on home preparations. A hospital bed and medical equipment had been requested. Home health care and physical therapy sessions were planned. I was going to have to do some rearranging of furniture to accommodate the "new furniture," but if Brian was coming home, I was prepared to do whatever necessary. Besides, I had enough help with my family.

I arrived the next day which was my birthday to spend time with Brian. We talked about him coming home. He asked me what I was going to do for my birthday, and I let him know I would spend most of the day with him. Later that evening our daughter and family had a birthday celebration planned with all my Mexican food favs prepared by my son-in-love. Brian and I joked he would have to go to Burgerville, a local hamburger fast food restaurant, because he couldn't eat the Mexican foods I loved. He was always talking about how he couldn't do spicy food. He made a deal with me though. Since I was leaving earlier to go to the celebration, I could bring him Olive Garden's lasagna the next day. When it came to keeping Brian happy, I was always going to get one of his cravings. On a few occasions, I went to several stores looking for glazed doughnut twists. Brian was insistent about having them, and I was glad I could oblige.

I didn't realize that this would be a birthday to remember. Within the next 24 hours, Brian's condition worsened with extreme pain and coughing. The last time I spoke with him was after I came home from the birthday celebration. We didn't talk long because he seemed tired.

I got ready to go back to the hospital the next day, but I had to wait for Olive Garden to open to make sure I brought his lasagna. I placed the order and picked it up. My phone rang as I was heading to the hospital. It was Sunday, the 4th of July. An oncologist asked if she was speaking to Brian's wife, and I confirmed. She introduced herself as the doctor on staff for the holiday and weekend. She asked me if I was planning to come to see him today, and I told her I was on my way. She said that she wanted to discuss Brian's condition currently and would wait until I arrived. My mind started racing because if she would wait for me to come before telling me, it probably was not good news. I silenced my thoughts and turned to pray. In my spirit, I knew the news was not good, but I prayed for God to continue to give me strength.

When I arrived at Brian's room, I couldn't believe how drastically he had changed from the day before. Nurses and a speech pathologist were working with him. The speech pathologist told me Brian couldn't speak. She encouraged me to talk to him because he could hear me. A few minutes later the oncologist who called me came in to talk to me.

We stepped aside, and she said she was very sorry to tell me that Brian had taken a turn for the worst. The lymphoma was not responding to the radiation treatment, and it was aggressively affecting his brain function. She said the prognosis this time was that they didn't believe Brian would live pass seventy-two hours. I was encouraged to have family members come and see him. She had ordered the restrictions of the number of visitors to be lifted. Brian was placed in "comfort care." They would do everything possible to make him comfortable and lessen the pain.

I wanted someone to lessen my pain. I had flashbacks of our lives together. The people we met, the places we traveled and lived, and most importantly how blessed we were to have a wonderful family. I remembered when the kids were growing up, Brian would tell them to always take care of each other because if they didn't, he would come back and haunt them. They would respond, "Dad," which is what they usually said when they thought he was kidding. I knew he meant it, and now I had to call each of them to have them come and see him.

All our kids came, each one cherishing their time with him. His best friend since childhood came and shared memories with him. When our second son came and talked to Brian about the basketball playoff games, he asked him who was going to win. He told him to blink once for the Milwaukee Bucks and twice for the Phoenix Suns. Brian blinked twice. We are big fans of football and basketball. Brian started that many years before. When our first son was born, Brian said, "I got myself a ball player!" All our kids played sports and now their kids are playing. I'm one proud "Mom Mom." They all promised they would look after each other. My oldest son said they would look after me too.

That evening, after they all left, I put on the healing music and scriptures. I remained at the hospital those last two nights. The nurse on duty encouraged me to rest, and they would be taking care of Brian.

I didn't fall asleep right away. I could see and hear the nurses attending to Brian. He was given morphine for the pain. I prayed until I fell asleep.

During the early morning hours of July 6th, I woke up and couldn't hear any coughing or moaning. I could only hear the music playing. I sat up and asked God to continue to give me strength because I felt in my spirit the final transition had happened. I walked over and could not see Brian's chest move. I pushed the nurse's call button, and they came in to verify that Brian was gone. I stood there after receiving their condolences in a moment of shock. How could this happen when we were preparing to bring him home?

I cried as I sat at his bedside. The body that lay there was his earthly vessel. He was now before the Lord. He had no more pain, but he was assured we would be alright afterwhile. I knew when the kids and the two oldest grandsons came, I had to be strong for them. The grandsons were experiencing death for the first time. We experienced such an outpouring of condolences from the staff members. The doctor, who a month earlier wanted me to prepare the family, said that Brian fought. He said he was amazed how much he improved from when he first came to the hospital. It was sad when his sister who lives in Virginia asked to see her brother. We remained with Brian until we all felt somewhat at peace. I was the last to leave. I kissed Brian on the forehead and said, "This will be a birthday to remember!" I told him I know how proud he was that everyone was #gilliamstrong. As the matriarch, I would continue to fulfill the legacy we talked about so many times in our lives together. My last words were, "I love you, Brian Gilliam!"

Months later, when I was talking to a dear friend, she said I had lost my heartbeat but my heart was still beating, which meant God had a purpose for me to fulfill.

REFLECTIONS

When did you know the final transition was upon you for your spouse
or loved one?

_____

_____

_____

_____

_____

_____

_____

Who was the person you could talk to or confide in?

_____

_____

_____

_____

_____

_____

_____

What thoughts went through your mind about the final transition?

_____

_____

_____

_____

_____

_____

_____

_____

_____

_____

CHAPTER SEVEN

My Journey – Going Through

I was and continue to be blessed. I have learned not to take anything for granted. I say, "I'm great and for that I'm grateful!" This is not a cliché, but I did learn that from the very first mentor I had in my life. She was also the person who said to me she would believe in me until I believed in myself. I believe God prepares us for what is going to happen in our lives. It's up to us to accept the preparation. I am eternally grateful to the people God put into my life. Each one had a specific role in my preparation. I am who I am today because of my faith and the people God placed in my life. Each one had a role in my personal development. It's because of my personal and spiritual development that I could go through this tough time in my life.

The days following Brian's transition, I chose not to go home for a few days. I stayed with my daughter and her family. My son-in-love said I could stay as long as I wanted. He even said I could stay permanently. I appreciated the offer, but I knew I would want to be back in my own place, and they didn't need a "mother-in-law" underfoot. I am not your typical or perceived "mother-in-law. I'll let you figure that out.

Now came the time to plan Brian's celebration of life service. My daughter and I wanted to follow his wishes to celebrate his life, not an occasion with a traditional funeral. Brian had a notebook with all I needed to follow to the letter of his wishes and business that I would do later. Other than his family, Brian's life was his military career, a mobile disc jockey, a Dallas Cowboys fan, and his love for Chevrolet Corvettes.

"Going through" was doing what needed to be done and remembering Brian wanted us to live our lives. While Brianna and I worked out all the details of Brian's celebration of life, we also had grandsons playing basketball in a tournament in Las Vegas. Arrangements for Brian's body had been arranged, and we ordered "#gilliamstrong" T-shirts for the family to wear to the celebration and silicone bracelets, which included our hashtag and Brian's initials, birthdate, and transition date.

We traveled to Vegas for the tournament to support and cheer on our grandsons. The oldest grandson and his team were successful in winning the championship for his age group. Although we were dealing with Brian's passing, we knew he would want us to be living our lives. I was glad to catch up with a dear friend whom I have known for three decades. She was a welcomed distraction for what was going on in my heart. We told stories of our lives together through the years, which included meeting in Germany. We laughed, and she was able to see everyone during our weekend stay in Las Vegas.

By this time, I had returned to my home. It was back to reality. When I returned after the tournament, we were only a couple of weeks from the celebration of life. My daughter and I went back to finalizing the plans. I remained strong and had assurance that so many people were praying for me and my family. I am very grateful for the outpouring of love and support from all over the country.

I knew Brian was pleased with the arrangements according to his wishes. It was a true celebration, non-traditional in a beautiful park setting with full military honors. We secured a shelter in the park with a lifelike picture of Brian waving while "DJ-ing" one of his events. He had a huge smile that was very welcoming for all who attended. Inside the shelter, we arranged tables with memorabilia from all areas of his life. There was a memory share box with cards for everyone to fill out their favorite memory of Brian. We had mementos of the bracelet and a bookmark with Brian's obituary. We also set up a continental style breakfast for our guests. Each of the tables were adorned with various photographs of Brian and beautiful flower arrangements from Katie. She is one of my daughter's closest friends and like another daughter to me.

The celebration started with the color guard conducting their honor of a fallen serviceman. The sound of taps being played was difficult. The precision of their presentation was something to witness. When I was presented with the American flag, the airman had tears in her eyes, and I was deeply touched. My dear friend, Christine, presided the celebration. The highlights of the celebration were the reflections shared by family members and friends. I was pleasantly surprised to see another one of Brian's best friends who came in from Virginia. He, along with Brian's other best friend, shared great memories of the "3 Amigos" that made us laugh and cry. After a video of Brian's life, me and my children stood before our family and friends to express our gratitude and love during this difficult time. Another one of Brian's wishes was to offer everyone an opportunity to secure their own eternity by accepting Jesus Christ as their personal savior. I offered the invitation and asked them to connect with one of my ministry friends and share their decision.

When I think back on this journey of "going through," I know where and from Whom my strength comes. I have a personal relationship with God. I am not talking about religion. I am talking about the essence of my life in the hands of God who created me and you. Just as I offered an invitation to family and friends to accept at

Brian's invitation, I am making the same invitation to you who are reading this book.

If you have never accepted Jesus as your personal Savior or maybe you are wanting to rededicate your life, I invite you now to say this prayer. I also encourage you to connect with like-minded people who will guide you. Your life will be transformed first by the renewal of your mind. I celebrate with you.

Please say this prayer out loud:

> *"Heavenly Father, I come before You now and ask You to come into my life. I believe that Your Son, Jesus was born, lived, and died for my sins. I repent of all things, known and unknown, that were not Your will for me. Today, I confess with my mouth and believe with my heart that You are Lord over my life. Come into my heart and create in me a heart for You. Jesus, You died for me. Starting now, I am living for You! In Jesus' name, amen!"*

I, along with other believers, celebrate your decision. As a matter of fact, all of heaven rejoices. You have taken the first step. Even though you might not fully understand what is happening, I can assure you that your life will never be the same.

It comes a time on this journey that a test of endurance will come. Stay tuned for the continuation of my journey with "Everyone has Gone Home - Enduring."

REFLECTIONS

What does "going through" mean for you?

_____

_____

_____

_____

How has the support of family and friends helped?

_____

_____

_____

_____

What part of "going through" was the toughest for you?

_____

_____

_____

_____

CHAPTER EIGHT

My Journey – Everyone has Gone Home – Enduring

Days after Brian's celebration of life service, I went through a gamut of emotions. After almost two years without seeing my siblings due to the pandemic, it was great spending time with them. My sister, Deborah, even came the very next day after Brian passed and returned for the celebration of life. I had my moments of sadness. For the most part, I immersed in the love, laughter, admiration, pleasure, joy, hopefulness, and care. Family and close friends came from all over the country. The times we were together were always memorable. The hardest part of getting together was going home. I would now have to rely on God for endurance.

I knew the reality of my "new" life without my "heartbeat" would be challenging at times. A flood of memories over four decades came to my mind during the times I was alone. I wanted to remain strong for my children and grandchildren. All of them handled grief differently. I encouraged them to share with me or their parents when questions came up. I also encouraged them to keep the memories of Brian going. We still talk about what he would do or say in different situations, and it makes us laugh.

There was never a time that my thoughts were of anything other than endurance. Endurance means to withstand hardship or adversity.

The opposite of endurance would be weakness or vulnerability. My emotions or feelings at times might be that of sadness because I truly miss Brian not physically being here or my family and friends leaving to go back home. The spirit of me knows that Brian is in a better place, and I stay close to my family and friends. God wants me to endure by rightly standing on His Word. I have the need for endurance so when I have done the will of God, I will receive the reward promised.

That's why my heartbeat is still going. I immediately sought ways to endure. I submersed myself into service. I am a personal shopper serving people by shopping and delivering to them. I love it because it is my pleasure to serve. I also have connected with other "Queen Warriors," women whose husbands have transitioned. We support each other by lending an ear to listen and encourage. Other projects are in the works at the writing of this book, more to come later. My children and grandchildren are so important to the essence of my life. As a child, I didn't have a relationship with my grandparents. I felt a void in my life, that I was robbed of that special bond. It was important for my children to have a relationship with their grandparents.

Unfortunately, they did not know Brian's parents because they passed away when they weren't born or too young. They knew my parents but because we were military only spent time with them on occasions like holidays or summer vacations. They still have memories of them they treasure.

I knew I wanted to be a part of my grandchildren's lives and create memories they would treasure into adulthood. I am blessed to have eleven "grandsugars" who are my "Why." I do what I do because they are the reason why I intentionally live to fulfill me and Brian's legacy for them. Brian told me to live my life. Now my life is for my children and grandchildren. I attend as many activities as possible they are involved in. I support them wholeheartedly.

I know that having a purpose to fulfill helps me to endure. As I mentioned, my children and grandchildren are my "Why." I heard this statement, and I keep it close by, "If you can look your why in the face and say, you're no longer reason enough; then you can quit!" I will not quit, give in, or give up. I couldn't look in their faces and ever say they aren't reason enough.

Every beat of my heart is intentional and has a purpose. I received a new revelation of the scripture in Psalm 30:5, Amplified, "Weeping may endure for a night, but a shout of joy comes in the morning." Some of my emotions are just for a moment. I have the favor of God always and joy is always with me. Each morning is a dawn of a new day God blesses us with to live and do His will.

REFLECTIONS

What thoughts or concerns have you had about when your family and friends leave?

_____

_____

_____

_____

_____

_____

_____

What plans do you have to "endure" during this time?

_____

_____

_____

_____

_____

_____

_____

_____

What is your "Why" for your life after your spouse or loved one is gone?

_____

_____

_____

_____

_____

_____

_____

_____

CHAPTER NINE

My Journey – Taking Care of Business

I n the midst of grieving the loss of my husband, there was business that needed to be conducted. Brian had a plan he had put into place over five years ago. This plan included his will, living trust, and powers of attorney for finances and health care. At the end of this book, there will be suggestions to assist you in making sure you are prepared with documents that will save you time and peace of mind.

I later discovered we are not always sure of what we will face during this time of conducting business on behalf of your spouse or loved ones. I do know that having a plan takes the guesswork out of it. I also recommend that you remain steadfast as an advocate for your spouse or loved ones. I would choose 1 to 2 people who are family members to assist you with decisions and be a great support for you.

I was blessed to have our daughter, Brianna, to assist me with decisions, and she was very supportive. As a matter of fact, she was the one who said her dad had something he was adamant about her signing as a notary when we were visiting for her wedding. Because she said that, I went on a hunt for the binder. Brian also had another binder that held all important documents such as our marriage license, birth certificates, military documentation, etc. He even kept the children's report cards in there.

I found the black binder, My Care Plan, in the same place as his red binder with all the other paperwork. A sigh of relief and gratefulness came over me that he had taken care of that for me. I asked myself why didn't I remember that binder at first, and realized we hadn't discussed his last wishes in over five years.

It is very important to have a conversation about the end of life with your spouse or loved ones. I know it's not a conversation that is easy to have, but it is necessary. I know how important it is, and I have had a conversation with my children about what to do when my transition happens. Otherwise, you are putting the surviving members of your family in an awkward situation. When details of the deceased final wishes are not legally prepared, the family could face delays in their estates.

I knew that having a team of professionals that could answer my questions was a big help. I also did my own due diligence in researching different situations that arose when doing business on Brian's estate. Some suggestions for a professional team would be legal representation, certified public accountant, and experienced tax preparer.

The first order of business was to follow his wishes outlined in his living trust. He wished to be cremated with a full military honors ceremony. Brianna and I researched businesses that conducted cremation, and found one that not only handled all details of the cremation, but also the military ceremony details. He was also entitled to have a marker at a national military cemetery. I was able to get certified death certificates through this company. Death certificates are needed when conducting business such as bank accounts, credit cards, insurance, etc.

Since Brian was a veteran of the Armed Services, there was business with government agencies. I had to notify financial services of his passing because he was collecting retirement. Also, Brian outlined there was an annuity for me as a surviving spouse that I was entitled to. The financial services department explained the process, but you have to remain steadfast when dealing with government agencies. It was a saga that no one should have to go through, but I am grateful that with persistence all was resolved.

It was during this process of conducting business that I realized I wanted to share my journey with others. My emotions were in check, especially since it seemed like every delay tactic was being used. I realized that we don't know what we don't know. Others can use that to their advantage if you just settle or back down. I was even told that they would have to put in a "hardship case" to expedite the process of me receiving what Brian had established for me. The perception of a "widow" is someone who is considered a "hardship case." As a "Queen Warrior," my faith said that greater is He who is in me that he who is in the world. The dignity of being a joint heir with Jesus and a child of the Most High, gives me strength to handle all that I needed and continue to do. I do recall saying to the person on the phone, "Whatever you need to do, do it." I also said that I didn't receive the title of a "hardship case" because God supplied all of my needs. I was entitled to what my husband established, and this was a disservice to his military career and memory. After that conversation, I received what I was entitled to the very next week! Thank you Lord!

I hope you can see why it is very important to have everything outlined in the necessary documents when faced with decisions for you and your loved ones. I understand that no one wants to think about their spouses or loved ones passing away. Talking about it is even harder. As a believer, I went through the emotions because Brian was no longer here physically. I miss our talks, our arguments, and even his

"Brian-isms," words he created. By faith, I see death also as life. Brian is in eternal life without pain or suffering.

We prepare for many transitions in our lives. We treasure births, weddings, graduations, sports accomplishments, etc. We avoid talking about death, maybe because we don't want it to happen. We all will transition one day. We are mortal beings with a date to be born and a date to transition by death. I encourage you to read the excerpt from the poem of " The Dash" at the end of this chapter. The "dash" is what you do between your born date and death date. I was a fan of this poem way back. Live your "dash" authentically with gratitude. It will be what people remember you for. Treasure everyday to the fullest. Take nothing for granted and then there won't be any regrets.

Talking about the wishes of your spouse or loved ones is a self-less act of caring by making sure their wishes are granted. Business will go on after they have passed on. Take steps to make sure those living on this side of heaven don't have to second guess what needs to be done.

The Dash Poem (Excerpt)
By Linda Ellis

I read of a man who stood to speak
At the funeral of a friend
He referred to the dates on the tombstone
From the beginning...to the end
He noted that first came the date of birth
And spoke the following date with tears,
But he said what mattered most of all
Was the dash between those years....

This poem is so very pertinent in our lives. I encourage you to search for this poem online and read it in its entirety. What is so important is what you do with the "dash." What does your "dash" look like?

REFLECTIONS

What steps have you taken to secure your family's future?

_____

_____

_____

_____

_____

_____

_____

_____

What legal paperwork has been completed for you and your spouse?

_____

_____

_____

_____

_____

_____

_____

_____

_____

What final requests have been documented?

_____

_____

_____

_____

_____

_____

_____

_____

_____

CHAPTER TEN

My Journey – Where do I go from Here?

Once everyone was home and my family was back to their lives of work and school, I had moments when I asked myself, "Where do I go from here?" Brian and I spent forty-six years of our adult lives together. We were just a few short years of that golden anniversary. Wow! I realize that is half a century with the same person. We were both the same person to each other physically, but we definitely weren't the same people emotionally, psychologically, mentally, etc. We lived our lives in constant seasons of life.

We spent the majority of our lives together with the exception of military assignments that sent Brian away. Even with those times, it was not longer than six months apart. Most people who know us were accustomed to seeing us together. I have never felt differently around family and friends since Brian's passing. I also have not seen my family and friends treating me differently.

Brian and I had talks during our marriage about our lives without each other, and we both agreed that life is for the living. The last five to ten years we talked about living our best life. I remember one conversation where Brian told me that I would move back to the west coast because at the time we lived in North Carolina if he passed before me. We laughed at the fact that he said I would be on the next thing smoking to get to Washington State. He also said that I would attend every sporting event or anything the "sugars" were involved in. I can definitely say that he knew me well. I love being apart of the "sugars" lives and creating memories with them. Yes, I am living my best life!

In our early years of marriage, the thought of being without Brian devastated me. The thoughts of death seemed to trap me into believing I couldn't go on without Brian. We never discussed how we deeply felt about being without the other, but it was something we just knew about each other. We also said that in living our lives, if we meet someone else, to not be afraid to fall in love again. At this time, I'm enjoying my life with my family and being in alignment with God's assignments for me. I enjoy companionship, and I believe that at an appointed time God will bring that person to me. Just like grief, there is not a timing or way a person should grieve or a timing to be with someone else. I love living my life according to God's will, not a person's timeline for me.

So, to answer the question of this chapter, I would say to live a great and grateful life. God has blessed me with gifts, talents, and strengths. All of my life's experiences have prepared me for where I am and where I am going. My life as a military wife took me away from what was "normal." I have come a long way from the woman who cried when I left my hometown of Hampton, Virginia. Most of the trip down Interstate 95 to Florida I cried because I was leaving my family.

My travels with Brian and our children not only gave me memories but experiences that I may not have had staying in my hometown. I rededicated my life to God and attended Bible teaching churches. I was a minister on staff where it wasn't about being qualified but being called. I have been a successful entrepreneur and businesswoman.

Remember when I said Brian and I both changed in so many ways, but we remained true to each other. I went from lacking confidence in myself to maturing in my relationship with God and gaining "God-fidence." I became a lifelong learner, and I'm living my life with purpose, power, and passion. The purpose of my life is to know my "WHY" for doing what I do. The power of my life is to have influence and impact with others by being in service to others with spiritual, practical concepts. The passion of my life is doing what I love and loving what I do.

The whole purpose of writing this book is to fulfill the purpose, power, and passion with others who are experiencing or experienced what I have. I will not settle for the perception of a "widow."

Here below is a table of the differences between "Widow" and "Queen Warrior." Feel free to compare the two and add your own thoughts.

WIDOW	QUEEN WARRIOR
Loss of Self	Knows her worth and value
Grief stricken/emotionally unstable	Experiences emotions but in control
Economically challenged	Economically strategizes for new lifestyle
Helplessness	Focuses on talents, gifts and strengths
Socially isolated	Secure in social relationships
Experiences Discrimination	A strong advocate for personal justice

In sharing this chart, I realized that very little has been written to help women to move forward from their loss. There are support groups, more are focused on handling the grief than how to go from here. It is my desire and goal to have a website and community for widows to queen warriors. Society pities "widows," but God wants us to know that we have value and worth.

During one of my studies and meditation times, I read Proverbs 31. This chapter in God's Word offers the best example of an ideal woman. It summarizes that the ideal woman is virtuous, strong, and selfless. She does not wait to be served, but rises early, even before sunrise, to delegate tasks and engage in business. She possesses a range of skills. She opens her heart to those in need. She is a loving person, dignified and her virtues increases her husband's reputation, and I include her husband's memory. She is sharp but honest, engaged in business for the benefit of her household. Above all this, a virtuous woman fears the Lord. A woman who fears the Lord is to be praised.

This is a celebration of who we are as women. We honor God by seeking Him in everything. We also trust Him with our hearts. This is where we receive spiritual maturity and wisdom. As a result, a Queen Warrior is dignified in her royalty and exhibits strength.

Our marriages enhance who we are as individuals. Whether you have been married several years or a few years, each husband and wife has their role. The husband is the head of the home, giving his life for his wife. The wife submits to her husband who lays his life down for her. Some women have a certain feeling about "submitting," but the best explanation I heard of submission is as a wife you come under the mission and offer support.

As Brian and I grew in our marriage, it was his role as my husband that helped me as a person and as his wife. He encouraged and supported me in all I attempted and achieved. He believed in me even in times when I didn't believe in myself. One thing he didn't grow out of was when I had to leave our home to travel for work. He would get very quiet taking me to the airport. He admitted to me that he knew I had to do what I did, but he missed me when I was away.

Am I trying to say that we had a perfect marriage? The answer is absolutely not. Just like other married couples, we had our share of differences. God blessed us for over forty years for a purpose. So as I go from here, our lives together, I am assured that God has a purpose for me, and my steps are so ordered. I am living my life and just being me!

REFLECTIONS

How have you imagined your life without your spouse or loved one?

_____

_____

_____

_____

_____

_____

_____

In what ways do you feel you were prepared for this season of your life?

_____

_____

_____

_____

_____

_____

_____

_____

_____

What is your purpose, power (influence), and passion for your life?

_____

_____

_____

_____

_____

_____

_____

_____

_____

CHAPTER ELEVEN

My Journey – Live Life: Just Being Me

My thoughts of living life are so much better than in my early years of being an adult. My younger years as an adult were years of being a wandering generality. I lacked confidence, was more of a follower than a leader, and settling for less than God's best. I was also a people pleaser, and even at times going against what I truly valued in order to be accepted by others.

When I met Brian, I learned valuable lessons throughout our years together. There's a saying about opposites attract, and the reason is a person sees qualities in another person that they lack. What a person lacks, they are drawn to a person because they would like to have certain qualities. While I had the qualities I mentioned before, Brian was the total opposite. He exhibited confidence, made decisions quickly, and rarely cared what people thought. He would tell me to believe in myself, give no one authority over you but God, and avoid being a people pleaser because you can't please everyone.

I eventually would meet other people in my life who helped me see how important it was to be the best version of myself, the person God created me to be. I remember learning about my personality and spiritual giftings through assessments. I would even take various assessments to see if I would come out differently. It would always be the same, and I enjoyed learning about me.

This was my first season of personal development, and throughout the years, I enjoyed becoming the best version of myself. I like to say that I am a lifelong learner, and the beauty of learning is that no one can ever take it away from you. I see the value in knowing who you are, why you are, and what being you means as far as your purpose for your life. Now, as a coach, I teach others about identifying their "best self." I also coach about practical concepts that leads a person to fulfilling their destinies through discipline in what I have learned over the years.

It is important to move from being a wandering generality to a mindful specific. I attribute all my life lessons and experiences to what I'm doing, the decisions I make, and the impact I have with those around me. I am also grateful for the Holy Spirit who dwells within me to guide me and teach me.

I truly believe that this version of me is how I am able to handle this season of my life. Everything in life is a season for us to learn from and become stronger for the seasons ahead of us. I can't imagine. If I would have decided to stop learning and growing, how would I have handled this season of my life?

Once I had the belief in myself, the next lesson was understanding what it meant to live a life of purpose. Through the years I have learned that living a purpose driven life is knowing your "WHY." Why are you here? Why are you doing what you do? Why have a purpose for your life? When I answered the "WHY" question earlier in my life, it was more of a selfish reason. It was much later when I realized that my "WHY" was to fulfill God's purpose for me through service to others. It was about finding what I truly was passionate about and pursue it with my whole heart. Today, my "WHY" is to be in alignment with the assignment God has given me to help others find their "WHY." I also add to that to create a legacy for my children's children of wealth and abundance.

God has given us power, love, and a sound mind. Your power is your influence that will impact the lives of others. Your passion, what you do with the least amount of effort, is what you will do for others. Together, the power and passion will give you the purpose driven life.

What you do on a daily basis will discipline you for your purpose. On a daily basis, I pray, meditate on the Word, read books, journal, speak affirmations, and I recently added afformations. I laugh and add value to whoever I can. I am inspired by positive people and then motivated from within to live on purpose.

This season of being without Brian has me discovering how to continue to live my best life without him. His words still ring in my ears to "live your life." One thing that is constant is knowing my "WHY" and the scripture in Jeremiah 29:11-12 (Amplified). The Amplified version states, "For I know the plans and thoughts that I have for you, says the Lord, plans for peace and well-being and not disaster, to give you a future and a hope. Then you will call on Me and you will come and pray to Me, and I will hear your voice and I will listen to you."

God has the plan for you and for me. When we discover our purpose, our steps are ordered. He promises a future and a hope. Spending time talking to Him, you are assured that He is listening to what you have to say.

Here are a few things I have learned in this season in order to live my best life:

1. Keep an attitude of gratitude and gratefulness. Never settle for good when great is available.
2. Spend time with my family. Even though I can never make up for the years we were apart in miles, I can live each day being

about them because they are my "WHY." Call, text, and Facetime just because.

3. Be in alignment with my assignment. I am to be a coach helping those discover their power, passion and purpose.

4. Take care of myself. Health and well-being are important so I can be around for my family.

5. Learn to live with myself. Spend time with me for reflection and direction. Remembering Brian through our memories. Find new hobbies that bring me fulfillment.

6. Maintain control of my life. Trust God completely.

7. Maintain short and long term actions for financial stability and legacy building.

8. Look for value in all relationships.

9. Create a community of women who have or currently are caregivers for spouses.

10. Be open to love again.

In this season of my life, I have learned so much, and I am so grateful for the opportunity to help others realize who they truly are much sooner than I did. What does living your life look like? Even though I shared my ten best life attributes, your list will look different, or we may share common thoughts about our best lives.

Now, I want to share some thoughts about what "just being me" means.

1. *Stop worrying about how other people see you.* Every person you know will have an opinion of who they think you are. Stop worrying about how they think. Chances are they aren't thinking about you as much as you believe they are.

2. *Who you are in "just being me" is enough.* We have a tendency in seeing ourselves less. Find three to five adjectives to describe

your "best self" and see yourself as enough. We do not have to measure up to other peoples' perceptions.

3. *You do not have to be a people pleaser.* Very seldom do I say that anything is impossible, but trying to please everyone leaves you lost in your own identity. Know your value and don't feel you have to measure up to others.

4. *Find out who you really are.* We are filled with all kinds of ideas of who we are supposed to be. Ask yourself, "Who Am I?" and search to find out.

5. *Be confident in who you are.* Everyone from time to time doubts or second guesses themselves. One way to "just be me" is to stop comparing yourself to others.

6. *Appreciate what makes you unique.* The Word states that we are created in the image of God. We are fearfully and wonderfully made. Our uniqueness sets us apart from others for a purpose (Psalm 139:14).

7. *Avoid being negative towards yourself.* If you find it hard for you to see the positive attributes of yourself, but find it easier to see what's wrong with you, you are expanding on what you focus on.

8. *Expect mistakes and learn from them.* The best way to do something right is to try, and if a mistake happens, you are learning what not to do in your quest.

9. *Strive for what you desire or have passion for.* Step out on faith and do what you love so you can love what you do. Passion is the ability to do what you love with the least amount of effort.

10. *Live your life with intention and purpose.* Someone should be able to see you living your best life because your thoughts and actions are aligned with who you are.

What I am sharing with you on this journey is what I have experienced in my life. Even after the passing of Brian, I knew that there was a purpose on the other side.

REFLECTIONS

How would you describe your "best life?"

_____

_____

_____

_____

_____

_____

_____

What do you do daily to be the best version of you?

_____

_____

_____

_____

_____

_____

_____

Which of the "just being me" statements resonates with you?

_____

_____

_____

_____

_____

_____

_____

CHAPTER TWELVE

My Journey – There's Purpose on the Other Side

God's Word states that the Lord made everything for its own purpose. (Proverbs 16:4, Amplified). Everything means everything. We may not understand what purpose some things have, but we have been created for a purpose. Every trauma and even drama was a part of the divine plan of purpose.

I don't know the answer, but I have wondered what purpose was it for Brian to live and love his family like he did and then die at a young age, especially when I can't help but notice other people who are so evil and tend to live long lives. I know I'm not the only one who had those thoughts when a loved one has passed on.

Later I realized that God has given us a specific purpose for each of us while on this earth, but once that purpose is done, we go home to be with our Lord. Brian's purpose was a provider and protector for our family. He supported me in my endeavors and always encouraged me to not give up. So, for those of us who are on this side of heaven, our purpose has four parts to it, which I created and shared with others.

The first part of pursuing our purpose is that we have a "PROMISE." As a matter of fact, we have over seven thousand promises in God's Word. We are to stand on those promises to fulfill our purpose. A couple of examples of scriptures from God's Word about promise are Joshua 21:45, Amplified, "God's promises never fail!" Another one is from Joshua 1:9, Amplified, God is always with me. "I command you to be strong and courageous - do not be afraid."

God designed us for a purpose. He has a plan of purpose for our lives and that's a promise in Jeremiah 29:11, Amplified, "For I know that plans and thoughts I have for you, says the Lord, plans for peace and well being and not for disaster, to give you a future and a hope."

Secondly, we have to trust the "PROCESS." How can you not trust the process when you have the promises? The process is what you do that will make the difference. Your steps have been so ordered by God. There will be times in the process when God gives you dreams, goals, and aspirations, and they will manifest suddenly. Other times, there is a waiting period. When you are waiting, God is preparing you for the dream, goal, or aspiration. By His Spirit, we are being taught during this time. Will you trust the "PROCESS?" I encourage you to read 1 Samuel 16. It is about David being anointed and appointed by God for a process. God has chosen us not because of our status, influence, or power. He chooses those who seek after His heart. He has the purpose plan or process backed by His promises. We get better in the process rather than get bitter.

Thirdly, there will be "PROBLEMS," or as I call them challenges. Problems are a part of the equation. Expect them and don't be caught off guard. They come our way to see how bad we want to pursue our dreams, goals, and aspirations. God knew we would encounter problems, and gave us promises for those problems. "The Lord is a refuge for those in times of trouble" (Psalm 9:9-10, Amplified).

Speak to your problems, "Why is it easy for me not to be moved by problems? Problems are a part of the process, and my promises will be fulfilled!" No one knows how long the problems will last. Just keep your mind on the promises.

Lastly, but certainly not the least, is the "PRIZE!" We all desire the prize. We may even like it if it was just handed to us. The prize is rewarded to the one who endures. You follow the process and overcome the problems because you have the promises. "Blessed is the man or woman who remains steadfast under trial, for when he/she has stood the test, he/she will receive the crown of life, which God has promised to those who love Him" (James 1:12, Amplified).

Do you see the importance of purpose? It's your DESTINY! Reaching your destiny will include the legacy you leave. I heard once if what you do is known by your first name, then it's about you. But if what you do is about others, then you are doing what you do by your last name. It's not just about you. Your destiny is what you are doing for others in your legacy.

We are a military family. Brian retired from the military. Our oldest son, Shawn is retired from the military, and our second son, Kevin, has over sixteen years in the military. I remember when both of them were considering a military career, Brian asked them what was the mission of the branch they chose. He told them they shouldn't choose a branch for the uniform because it wouldn't sustain them for an entire career. "You choose based on whether you can support the mission of the branch. Every branch has a specific mission." When I heard this, I thought that could apply to civilians as well. Thus, having a personal mission statement is important in your plan of purpose.

A personal mission statement is a written declaration and description of your purpose. It identifies who you are, what you do, who you do it for, and why you do it. This mission statement is about everything you do. From time to time you ask yourself, "Is this part of my purpose?" It allows you to live intentionally and on purpose.

In closing, I purposed myself by the leading of the Holy Spirit to share my journey with others, to encourage, educate, and empower you with your own journeys. I hope you have been enlightened and feel that you can elevate to the purpose God has for you. There is a sign in my office that reads, " Enjoy the Journey!" For many years, I told people there is JOY in the JOurneY. Joy is not a feeling or emotion you have when all is well. This joy I have, in spite of the challenges of my journey, is with me at all times. The joy of the Lord is my strength!

Rise up Queen Warriors! Remember, you are dignified with strength. Your position is strong and secure. Smile at your future because when you endure, you will receive your crown of life. Amen!

REFLECTIONS

What does intentionally living mean to you?

_____

_____

_____

_____

_____

_____

What is your purpose on this side of your life without your spouse or loved one?

_____

_____

_____

_____

_____

_____

_____

Write a personal mission statement identifying the who you are, what you do, who you do it for, and why.

_____

_____

_____

_____

_____

_____

_____

Resources

- Join a support group – Hospitals and funeral homes may have recommendations for these groups. (Queen Warriors Support Group to be announced)
- Social Security Administration – www.ssa.gov/survivors – Read about the Survivors Benefit, how to apply for the benefit, how to claim the one-time benefit usually associated with funeral or burial expenses
- Defense Finance Accounting Services – for those whose spouses are or were in the military or government employment
- Consult an attorney
- Hire a Certified Public Accountant
- AARP – resources for caregivers, articles of grief, bereavement, and mourning, death checklist, etc.
- Your church
- Insurance companies – policyholders notification of death

Checklist To Accomplish When Your Spouse Passes

_____Contact your legal representative. Laws vary from state to state. Ask family and friends if they have any recommendations for legal representation. They can help with the laws of your state.

_____Locate the last will and testament for living trust and final wishes for funeral or celebration of life. If there is no will, an attorney can help with the laws of the state for disbursements.

_____Contact the Social Security Administration. You may be eligible for survivor benefits. Call or visit to report your spouse's death.

_____Contact Defense Finance Accounting Services if your spouse was associated with the military or federal government employment.

_____Notify your spouse's employer. There may be life insurance policies, retirement, or 401(k) accounts.

_____Get copies of the death certificate. Originals will cost you. Some businesses require an original, others will take a photocopy.

_____Be sure to contact all life and health insurance companies.

_____Contact all financial companies about accounts. You should receive money from single accounts if you are listed as the beneficiary.

_____Talk with your tax preparer or accountant. They will advise how you will file for the current tax year and subsequent years.

_____Talk with a financial advisor. Get your affairs in order for your children and grandchildren.

Family Memories

Brian and Karen-Retro

The Gilliam Family

Brian and Gail

Brian's Leather Couch

Brian and Karen

Brian's Military Uniform

Brian, Karen and their children

This heart was in the carpet done by the Shark Robot.
I believe it was a message from Brian because he loved vacuuming.

Journal Entries
(November 2020 – December 2021)

Here are a few of my journal entries during my journey as Brian's caregiver. I randomly chose these entries to share. As I mentioned in chapter four, I kept a journal to reflect on the day, to keep an attitude of gratitude, and strengthen my memory. Now, it is documented, and I can refer to it from time to time.

Other benefits of writing and keeping a journal are to reduce stress and anxiety, to be a form of inspiration, to help achieve goals, and to track progress. There are many types of journals: gratitude, thoughts, dreams, food, fitness, and goals. You may even find that you have a specific reason for keeping a journal, and I encourage you to go with it.

11/2/20

Father, I am grateful you are the center of my life. Nothing catches you by surprise. I pray for Your strength in what lies ahead for Brian and I. I will rely and stand on your Word. I am allowing my faith to become greater than my fears. It's the uncertainty, which is a form of fear. You have not given me the spirit of fear, but of love, power and a sound mind. As Jesus is in heaven, so I am in this world. I am Your righteousness. Through Christ, I can do all things. I speak life and life more abundantly. I pray for Brian and his health. No weapon formed against us will prosper. In Jesus' name, amen.

12/31/20

Father, I cry out to You! Your name is above this pandemic. I declare that by Jesus' stripes Brian and I are healed. I curse the symptoms in my body. I speak divine health and that Your promises will manifest in 2021. Thank You, Lord!

4/4/21

Father, I shout Hallelujah! I am so grateful that Brian has had his last chemo treatment. Today, he rang the bell in victory! Thank you, Lord, for keeping us and sustaining us through this trial. I pray for continued strength for Brian in his recovery.

7/3/21

Here I am, Lord, at 64 years of age! I'm here in Brian's hospital room where he has been for the last month. My hope is in You, the author of my faith. I keep speaking life and am not moved by what I see with my natural eyes. You sent Your Word and healed them. I believe in Brian's healing. In Jesus' name, amen.

12/18/21

First Anniversary Without You

I knew this day would come and I knew I would have to prepare,
The day we exchanged our vows forty-four years ago today.
That day and many more you took my breath away,
And now I breathe without you each and every day.
I have the memories and our family's love,
I am at awe at God's Hand from above.
I loved you the day we wed,
I was always right by your side where you were led.
The bond is strong and I know you are at rest,
The day we will reunite will be the best.
Until that time I will lead this family with your spirit of love within me.
Happy Anniversary Brian!

Love Always,

Karen

About the Author

Karen Gilliam, also known as Coach KG, is a CIO, Continuously Inspiring Others, leader in the professional and private sectors. She uses her strengths of communication, winning others over, being a maximizer, showing empathy and positivity to coach others to be the best version of themselves. She encourages women to design their lives and not live by default.

She takes her life experiences and shares spiritual and practical disciplines to execute for the best outcomes. The journey as her husband's caregiver was the most challenging to date. During her journey of caregiving and her husband's passing, Karen relied on her faith and family to carry her through.

She shares this journey with those who may be going through the same journey or to prepare others for what may lie ahead. She is always wanting to help others to be better when faced with adversity.

Karen has been a speaker, teacher, coach, and businesswoman for over four decades. She is currently preparing for a Queen Warriors support group. She resides in Vancouver, WA with her family. Karen enjoys crafting, completing word and trivia games, cooking, and creating memories for her children and "grandsugars."

His Glory Creations Publishing, LLC is an International Christian Book Publishing Company, which helps launch the creative fiction and non-fiction works of new, aspiring and seasoned authors across the globe, through stories that are inspirational, empowering, life-changing or educational in nature, including poetry, journals, children's books, and recipe books.

DESIRE TO KNOW MORE?

Contact Information:
CEO/Founder: Felicia C. Lucas
www.hisglorycreationspublishing.com
Email: hgcpublishingllc@gmail.com
Phone: 919-679-1706

Made in United States
Troutdale, OR
06/06/2024

20363288R00059